POEMS FROM THE MEDIATIZED SOULSCAPE

j. martin strangeweather

All rights reserved. No part of this book may be reproduced or transmitted in any form or by any means, electronic or mechanical, without written permission from the author. All requests should be sent to: jmartinstrangeweather@gmail.com

Cover artwork by J. Martin Strangeweather
Graphic design by Dustin Myers
Published by the Santa Ana Literary Association
Santa Ana, CA 92701
Printed in the United States of America
ISBN 978-0-578-28847-5
Library of Congress Control Number: 2022906651
Copyright © 2022 by J. Martin Strangeweather

for the Morlocks and the Eloi,

and our future A.I. cybercrats

Media + Hypnotized = Mediatized

Mediatized realism is akin to surrealism and magical realism, but with a distinctly North American twist. Whereas surrealism originates from Europe and focuses on the unsettling materializations of the subconscious in our conscious world, and magical realism hails from Latin America and explores the collective manners in which the subconscious becomes matter-of-factly translated into the conscious world, mediatized realism is centered on the methods and strategies by which certain agents very consciously refashion the subconscious landscape through mass media and social media. Surrealism presents commonplace events such as dreams and Freudian slips as deviant manifestations of fantastical psychological processes occurring in secrecy. In Magical realism, the reader is led to accept fantastical events as a normal part of everyday life. Mediatized realism doggedly calls attention to the corporate and political reconstruction of our psyche. Surrealism and magical realism tend to withhold information from the reader. Mediatized realism tends to overload the reader with information.

Factoid #1

In 1928, Edward Bernays, American pioneer of propaganda, published his seminal work, *Propaganda*, in which he argues that public relations plays a crucial role in establishing/maintaining societal order. Here is an excerpt from the book: "The conscious and intelligent manipulation of the organized habits and opinions of the masses is an important element in democratic society. Those who manipulate this unseen mechanism of society constitute an invisible government which is the true ruling power of our country. We are governed, our minds molded, our tastes formed, and our ideas suggested, largely by men we have never heard of… it is they who pull the wires that control the public mind."

I-Brain

You think more with your I-Brain
than your real brain.
Don't pretend you don't.

Your real brain
is the I-Brain.
Don't pretend it isn't.

The I-Brain is not
an extension of you.
You are an extension of
the I-Brain.

The Malady

We used to just watch people on the screen.
Now we are the people on the screen.
Now we are the screen,
and everyone's an advertisement
for their own brand
of desperation.*

*The more time one spends interacting with/through screen-based media, the less responsible one will feel for engaging in the social norms (politeness, respectfulness, attentiveness, etc.) that accompany face-to-face interaction. As one becomes less able to display the social norms necessary to conduct positive (or even neutral) face-to-face interactions, one will increasingly spend time in isolation, experiencing reality vicariously through a screen specifically filtered and attuned to their particular sensibilities, making them less and less able to participate in meaningful/healthy face-to-face interactions.

More Cake, Please

Swiping to the left of what's left to swipe,
I come across the pretty face
of the woman of my dreams.
I come across the pretty face,
the pretty face on the screen.

Her name is Orpah Dorpa Ling,
which is Phonysian for
"one-legged goat milker from the Hills of Ling."
I know this because I speak Phonysian fluently.
I'm part Phonysian.
Most Southern Californians
have Phonysian blood in them.

We meet at Jack's Bistro.
She doesn't look anything like her picture.
There's no frame around her,
and she's not made of pixels,

though she does seem two-dimensional.

Orpah orders a microphone and a film crew.
I order breadsticks.
They come right away,
fresh from the oven, piping hot.
Not the breadsticks, the film crew.

"Look under your chair," says Orpah.
"Huh?"
"Surprise!" she says.
"For participating in tonight's date,
everyone gets a Samsung Galaxy IQ smartphone!"

"Um…"

All the diners are looking under their chairs,
squealing and oinking with delight as they hold up
their brand-new Samsung Galaxy IQ smartphones,
still in the package.

"Bachelor Number One," says Orpah,
reading from her cue card,
"who were you fantasizing about
the first time you masturbated?"
The cameraman zooms in on my face.

"Er…"

The waiter comes with two baskets of breadsticks
and sets them on the table.
"Only one of these is real," he says.
"The other is a cake.
Which one is real
and which one is fake?"

"Uh…"

I have no patience for dating games.
I choose the one
that looks like a basket of breadsticks.

"Surprise!" says Orpah.
"They're both made of cake!
It's all cake! Everything's cake!
Have yourself a sweet slice of life!"

I grab the cake knife
and stick it in the waiter's gut.
She isn't exaggerating.
The waiter is cake.
I flip the table over,
only to discover that it's cake, too—
hazelnut marzipan
with a vanilla fondant tablecloth.
I check to see if my date is cake,
slicing her in half, right down the middle.
Her raspberry cream filling
oozes onto the floor.
The floor itself is made of cake,
a dry, run-of-the-mill chocolate.

Slicing further downward,
I split our four-layer planet in twain,
exposing the whole world's cakey fakery.

Everything and everyone
is mostly just frosting.

Having had my fill of the spectacle,
I plunge the knife deep inside my chest,
and cut myself a slice.
Did I mention I'm cake, too?

We're all moist and delicious cakes,
ooey and gooey and decadently rich.
We can't help but devour one another.
It's a cake eat cake world.

Exploring the mediatization of this poem:

1. The author had been binge-watching *Is it Cake?* on Netflix at the time of this poem's creation.
2. The author's spouse made a comment which incorporated the dating app idiom of "swiping to the left" at the time of this poem's creation.
3. The poem starts with a man looking at a screen in the pursuit of fulfillment.
4. The narrator's date's name is a not-so-subtle variant of Oprah, calling to mind Oprah Winfrey, a famous talk show hostess.
5. Jack's Bistro is a reference from the television show *Three's Company*, which was set in Santa Monica, California.
6. The poem incorporates elements of the television game shows *The Dating Game* and *Is it Cake?* Surreal connections can be made between the two shows.

7. The poem is written in a manner which incorporates cinematic special effects to literary ends, i.e., mediatized realism.
8. The poem is constantly alluding to the manufactured experience of our life, the Hollywoodization of our consciousness.
9. "Having had my fill of the spectacle…" is a reference to Guy Debord's *The Society of the Spectacle* (1967).

Factoid #2

American novelist and political critic Mary McCarthy on mass media manipulation: "The Nixon success, if it's really serious, is too horribly Orwellian to contemplate; it would mean that mass society is a reality, which nobody here, even those who have denounced its symptoms, really has ever believed except in talk. The idea that people are influenced, not by their passions or interests, but by advertising techniques, i.e., by mass-conditioning, blows all my conceptions of U.S. life sky-high." This quote is from 1952. Needless to say, no one is shocked by the idea of mass media programming/conditioning any longer, which itself should be shocking, though it is not. We have grown numb from psychic abuse.

Mediatized

I'm down in Plato's cave, strapped into my seat, looking up at the projection screen, watching the Titanic sinking in monochrome, the Hindenburg nosediving in Technicolor, the Death Star exploding in VistaVision, E.T. phoning home, Mel Gibson pretending to be William Wallace shouting, "Freedom!" with his dying breath, Tom Hanks sitting on a bench, remarking that, "Life is like a box of chocolates," Kirk Douglas standing up and declaring, "I'm Spartacus!" Humphrey Bogart consoling Ingrid Bergman with the line, "We'll always have Paris," Ralph Macchio telling Ponyboy to "stay gold," Al Pacino chanting, "Attica!" Marlon Brando in a ripped shirt yelling, "Stella!" Meg Ryan faking an orgasm in a crowded restaurant, Jimmy Stewart desperately pleading, "I want to live again!" Sean Connery and Roger Moore saying their name is Bond, James Bond, Clint Eastwood threatening some punk to go ahead and make his day, Judy Garland admitting to her dog, "I have a feeling we're not in Kansas anymore," Charlton Heston commanding Yul Brynner to let his people go, Jack Nicholson dressed in a colonel's uniform, stating matter-of-factly that we can't handle the truth, Charlie Chaplin imitating Hitler, Bugs Bunny in drag seducing Elmer Fudd, Richard Attenborough welcoming the audience to Jurassic Park, Gene Kelly singing in the rain, Julie Andrews twirling on a mountaintop, Slim Pickens riding an atom bomb to ground zero, a gusty subway grate blowing up Marilyn Monroe's white dress and showing off her shapely legs, Anthony Perkins stabbing Janet Leigh in the shower, Cary Grant fleeing from a crop duster, Sylvester Stallone running up some stairs in a sweatshirt and sweatpants, seven astronauts strutting down a corridor, seven diamond thieves and one undercover cop ambling through a parking lot, John Cleese walking very silly, Uncle Ben warning Tobey Maguire, "Remember, with great power comes great responsibility," Robert De Niro looking in the mirror and asking, "You talkin' to me?"

Immobilized by eidetic tentacles of cinema,
even the simplest expressions of freedom
are extremely difficult,
requiring an extraordinary effort
of concentration
and willpower.

The Revolution Will Be YouTubed

the revolution will be no re-run, brothers
the revolution will be live [1]

a revolution is a struggle
between the future and the past [2]

oh, the movie never ends
it just goes on and on
and on
and on [3]

a diamond is forever [4]

---

[1] Gil Scott-Heron
[2] Fidel Castro
[3] Journey
[4] De Beers

ideas are more powerful than guns
we would not let our enemies have guns
why should we let them have ideas [5]

i actually don't like thinking
i think people think i like to think a lot
and i don't
i do not like to think at all [6]

have it your way [7]

---

[5] Joseph Stalin
[6] Kanye West
[7] Burger King

i'm the object of criticism around the world
but i think that since i am being discussed
i am on the right track [8]

everyone is entitled
to my opinion [9]

don't leave home without it [10]

---

[8] Kim Jong Il
[9] Madonna
[10] American Express

just do it [11]

i want you to know that everything i did
i did for my country [12]

i'm the tool of the government
and industry too
for i am destined to rule
and regulate you [13]

there is freedom of speech
but i cannot guarantee freedom
after speech [14]

there are some things money can't buy [15]

---

[11] Nike
[12] Pol Pot
[13] Frank Zappa
[14] Idi Amin
[15] Mastercard

the beam becomes my dream
my dream is on the screen [16]

by the skillful and sustained use of propaganda
one can make a people see even heaven as hell
or an extremely wretched life as paradise [17]

they might be better off i think
the way it seems to me
making up their own shows
which might be better than T.V. [18]

---

[16] Blondie
[17] Adolf Hitler
[18] Talking Heads

Factoid #3

American inventor Philo T. Farnsworth invented the television. Here's what he had to say about his most famous invention: "There's nothing worthwhile on it, and we're not going to watch it in this household, and I don't want it in your intellectual diet."

How to Read a Circular Book

...craving, craving, craving,
it was the best of times
if you read between the lines,
it was the worst of times
if you read between the lines,
craving, craving, craving,
we the readers of the United States,
in order to form a more perfect understanding
of what it means to read between the lines,
craving, craving, craving,
literary theorists shall make no law
respecting an establishment of
singular interpretation,
or prohibiting the free exercise thereof;
or abridging the freedom to read between the lines,
craving, craving, craving,
reading between the lines does not delight
in confusion

but rejoices with the truth,

craving, craving, craving,

there is nothing either good or bad between the lines

but thinking makes it so,

craving, craving, craving,

as the reader awoke one morning

from troubled dreams,

he found himself transformed

into something that could only be deciphered

by reading between the lines,

craving, craving, craving,

she would've been a good reader

if there had been somebody there

forcing her to read between the lines

every minute of her life,

craving, craving, craving,

what we talk about

when we talk about reading between the lines,

craving, craving, craving,

I am he as you are he as you are me and we are all

reading between the lines,

desperately craving,

fearfully craving,

maddeningly craving,

that's one small step for man,

one giant leap for those who know how to read between the lines,

craving this, craving that, craving more…

The Eidos of Transtextual Telepathy

I'll become you, the person reading this text,
and you'll become me, the text.

We are synthesized,
you and me.
Your mind is receptive to my verbal illusions.

If I say envision a white unicorn,
you will envision a white unicorn.
And if I say envision Albert Einstein
wearing a big red clown nose,
you will envision Albert Einstein
wearing a big red clown nose.

But something very mysterious just happened.
Aside from the red clown nose,
did you imagine him in black and white,
as a memory stolen from an old photo,

or did you imagine him in living color?
Did he have a serious expression on his face?
Was he wearing a sweater or a lab coat,
or did you skip his outfit altogether?

How much of him did you create
for yourself to see?
Did you include his shoes?
I'll bet you didn't.
Were parts of him indistinct,
even formless?

Reinterpreted and retranslated,
you are the page,
and I am reading you.

a ghostly chorus of algorithms

change the channel
and channel something different

turn the dial
alter the brainwave
and tune into someone different

the static between channels
is speaking in electronic tongues

there is no turning back
there is no reconnection

so what do you connect with
when you disconnect?

a theory is not a home
and conspiracies make an unrestful bed
but it will have to suffice

Gridlocked

Don't kid yourself.
Disconnection is impossible.
You can't live off-the-grid.
You are the grid.
The grid is you.

The grid runs on psychosocial energy.
You were born of the grid.
You carry the grid wherever you go.

Q: Why did the conformist cross the road?
A: Because mass media told him to.

Q: Why did the nonconformist cross the road?
A: Because mass media told him not to.

Conclusion: No matter what you do,
there's no escaping mass media's influence.

Politics won't free you.
Religion won't free you.
Wealth and status won't free you,
and neither will Slab City.
Alcohol and drugs help
temporarily,
but if you aren't careful,
you'll become even more addicted
to the grid.

The grid extends to the edge
of the known universe.

Factoid #4

On average, there are sixteen minutes of commercials for every hour of programming. The average U.S. child spends an average of six hours per day watching television, exposing them to ninety-six minutes of commercials every day. This means the average U.S. child has spent well over five thousand hours downloading consumerist propaganda into his or her receptive brain by the time they are ten years of age—well over five thousand hours of deceptive advertising tactics drilled into their defenseless minds during the formative years, and this is only the commercials, to say nothing of the dubious content of the programs they are watching *between* the commercials.

Medea and the Fool's Gold Fleece

Medea was a sorceress
who betrayed her people
and murdered her children.

Mass Medea is an illusionist
who enslaves her people
and steals her children's souls.

Sims of Sims

Ask yourself:
Why do I believe the things I believe?

The not-so-right answer:
I believe the things I believe
because the things I believe are correct.

The righter answer:
I believe the things
I have been conditioned to believe
because the things
I have been conditioned to believe
have not totally failed me yet.

The rightest answer:
Everything I believe is false,
but I am generally in denial,
and anyway,
the show must go on.

The Matrix Squared

Take a moment to look all around you.
Notice how the landscape is overwhelmed
with human thoughts
turned concrete.

Some of us programs
wonder if we're living in a simulation.
Of course we're living in a simulation,
in at least two distinct manners:
sensorially & conceptually,
both of which simulate limited versions
of a vaster reality
not fully perceived & comprehended.
What would computerized simulation
add to this equation?

And if reality is computer generated,
who's to say the reality behind the simulation
is not itself a simulation,
and so on,
ad infinitum?
It's enough to realize that
reality is a psychosocial construct.
Everything is ideation/hallucination/simulation.

Factoid #5

American economist Robin Hanson has some strangely pragmatic advice for anyone who believes they are living in a computerized simulation: characters in a high-fidelity simulation should strive to be entertaining and praiseworthy in order to avoid being switched off, cancelled, or relegated to the role of a semiconscious (or even nonconscious) low-fidelity NPC (non-player character).

Beyond the Infinity Mirror's Illusion

Whether or not I am supersymmetric strings
and photons
and quarks
and atoms
and molecules
and microscopic cells
and electrochemical synapses
and subconscious impulses
(and perhaps even soul stuff)
in a brain
in a holographic simulation
in a hyperdimensional superposition
of the multiversal wavelength,
I am still sitting at the desk in my room,
writing this poem.

In plainest words,
I am the concept
of me,
and the familiar feeling
of that concept.

Cinematic Oracle

Which movie would you rather watch:
the one where the crisis is easily averted
by everyone working together as equals,
or the one where the hero saves the day
and the bad guy gets what's coming to him
after lots of bang-bangs and boom-booms?

I already know your answer.
It's my answer, too.
That's why we're doomed.
The ratings are our rulers now.

sanity (noun): the ability to think and behave in a normal and rational manner; sound mental health.

According to whom?

> *the Nazis?*

>> *the Spanish inquisitors?*

the Sicilian Mafia?

>> *the Scientologists?*

the Donald Trump fanatics?

> *the Quakers?*

> *the Mormons?*

> *the atheists?*

the psychological community?

> *your local community?*

the commercials on television?

Everyone in every era is un-sane,
and the most sane behavior one can partake in
is to study our various modes of un-sanity.

If the rules and restrictions
(the guidelines?)
of sanity
are based on that which makes a society flourish
over the long term,
then it is clear that every modern-day society
is inflicted with multiple strains
of insanity.

Surreal is the New Real

The president of Ukraine is on the big screen
pleading for aid
against a powerful oppressor.

(insert laugh track here)

Thousands of kilometers away,
a roomful of politicians in expensive suits
give the president on the big screen
a standing ovation.

(insert laugh track here)

I watch it all from the safety of my television
wondering what's new on Netflix.

(insert laugh track here)

The Antidote Is In the Poison

This poetry collection
was brought to you
by the wonders
of modern technology.

Mass media isn't just them anymore.
Mass media is me.
Mass media is you.

If you can't escape the screen,
you can at least become
your own content creator,
your own reality T.V. show,
your own movement.
But to what end?

"Careful," warn all the gods
and goddesses
as you walk in their fading footsteps.

It's a DIY world.
Heck, it's a DIY universe.
It always has been.

A Mediatized Realist Watchlist

The King of Comedy (1982)
Tron (1982)
Videodrome (1983)
Brainstorm (1983)
1984 (1984)
The Running Man (1987)
They Live (1988)
Total Recall (1990)
Closet Land (1991)
Quiz Show (1994)
The Cable Guy (1996)
The Truman Show (1998)
Pleasantville (1998)
eXistenZ (1999)
The Matrix (1999)
Adaptation (2002)
Idiocracy (2006)
Surrogates (2009)
Scott Pilgrim vs. the World (2010)
The Hunger Games (2012)
Ready Player One (2018)
WandaVision (2021)
Free Guy (2021)

Andy Kaufman interview with David Letterman:
https://www.youtube.com/watch?v=6p0sr2BejUk

In the future you will know my computer-generated avatar by his golden-scaled skin and silver dreadlocks stretching to the ground and trailing three kilometers behind him. You will know my avatar by his two-pronged silver beard streaked with rainbows, and his hypnotic licks of orange flame for eyes. My avatar will wander the simulated world(s) unclothed, dispensing half-moon secrets and solar eclipse mysteries, his nakedness forever pixelated. He will be so much more than me, and so much less.

J. Martin Strangeweather believes we are often mistaken about what we believe. His work has appeared in numerous publications, but who cares? Sometimes he refers to himself in the third person, like now, for instance. To learn more, please visit: www.jmartinstrangeweather.com

www.ingramcontent.com/pod-product-compliance
Lightning Source LLC
Chambersburg PA
CBHW032018290426
44109CB00013B/705